EYEWITNESS DISASTER
FLOODS!

HELEN DWYER

W

FRANKLIN WATTS
LONDON•SYDNEY

First published in 2010 by Franklin Watts

Copyright © 2010 Arcturus Publishing Limited

Franklin Watts
338 Euston Road
London NW1 3BH

Franklin Watts Australia
Level 17/207 Kent Street, Sydney, NSW 2000

Produced by Arcturus Publishing Limited,
26/27 Bickels Yard, 151–153 Bermondsey Street, London SE1 3HA

Planned and produced by Discovery Books Ltd., 2 College Street, Ludlow, Shropshire, SY8 1AN www.discoverybooks.net
Managing editor: Rachel Tisdale
Editor and Author: Helen Dwyer
Designer: sprout.uk.com Limited
Maps: Stefan Chabluk
Picture researcher: Tom Humphrey

Photo acknowledgements: Corbis: 8 (Stephen Hird/Reuters), 19 (Piyal Adhikary/epa), 20 (Murad Sezer/Reuters), 21 (Miller/Reuters), 24 (Roland Scheidemann/dpa), 26 (Momatiuk – Eastcott). Discovery Photo Library: 23. Geohazards.info: 22 (James Searle). Getty Images: cover (Arif Ali/AFP), 4 (STR/AFP), 5 (Andrew Yates), 9 (Per-Anders Pettersson/Prestige), 11 (Craig Lassig/AFP), 12 (Patrick Lin/AFP), 17 (Munir Uz Zaman/AFP), 18 (STRDEL/AFP), 27 (Sena Vidanagama/AFP). Shutterstock: 6 (pinecone), 7 (Lumir Jurka), 13 (Alex Neauville), 15 (Claudio Bertoloni), 28 (fotoJoost), 29 (Marc Pinter). US Air Force: 10 (Master Sgt Paul Gorman). Wikimedia: 14 (Thorfinn Stainforth).

Cover picture: Pakistani people wade through a flooded street after a heavy downpour in Lahore, 13 July 2006.

Sources
http://www.jaha.org/edu/flood/story/victor_heiser-flood-desc.html *page 6*
http://www.people.com/people/archive/article/0,,20118116,00.html *page 7*
http://news.bbc.co.uk/1/low/world/africa/657209.stm *page 8*
http://www.channel3000.com/news/16559796/detail.html *page 10*
http://gazettextra.com/news/2008/jun/09/lake-delton-empties-out/ *page 10*
http://www.thehawkeye.com/Story/flood-Keithsburg-061508 *page 11*
http://dissidentvoice.org/Feb06/Quigley21.htm *page 13*
http://news.bbc.co.uk/1/hi/talking_point/4146031.stm *page 14*
Middleton, Nick. Going to Extremes, Pan Books, 2003 *page 16*
http://www.ecoearth.info/shared/reader/welcome.aspx?linkid=103408 *page 17*
http://news.bbc.co.uk/1/hi/world/south_asia/6927389.stm *page 18*
http://observer.guardian.co.uk/world/story/0,,2141849,.html *page 18*
http://www.actionaid.org/india/index.aspx?PageID=3554 *page 18*
http://www.redorbit.com/news/general/1040130/storm_flooding_moves_into_ohio/index.html *page 21*
http://news.bbc.co.uk/1/hi/uk/3577714.stm *page 22*
http://news.bbc.co.uk/1/hi/england/cornwall/3571984.stm *page 23*
http://www.geoprojects.co.uk/Keyfile/KeyBoscastle.htm *page 23*
http://www.nwf.org/news/story.cfm?pageId=5C273840-5056-A868-A07C0D986E86BF10 *page 27*
http://ecomedia.org.au/press/category/various/page/9/ *page 27*
http://www.nytimes.com/2005/09/06/science/06tech.html?pagewanted=all&ex=1283659200&en=f2cbac7c075230ad&ei=5090&partner=rssus erland&emc=rss *page 28*

Words in **bold type** or underlined appear in the glossary on page 30.

CONTENTS

What is a flood? 4

Coping with a flood 6

Heavy rain and river floods 8

'It looked like a giant waterslide.' 10

Cyclones and hurricanes 12

Tsunamis and high tides 14

Monsoon floods 16

*'There were many poisonous
snakes in the water.'* 18

Flash floods 20

*'There were cars all around
us at sea.'* 22

Manmade floods 24

Floods and global warming 26

Flood prevention 28

Glossary 30

Further information 31

Index 32

WHAT IS A FLOOD?

A flood is simply a large quantity of water covering land that is normally dry. This usually happens after heavy rainfall, but earthquakes, high tides and even human activities can also cause floods.

Most flooding occurs around low-lying rivers. The flat area next to a river is called a **flood plain**. When a river is so full it can hold no more water, it spills onto this flood plain.

In August and September 2009, many countries in western Africa were hit by severe flooding. This is Ouagadougou, the capital of Burkina Faso, where 150,000 people had to leave their homes and find shelter.

Floods and farming

For thousands of years, farmers have depended on seasonal river floods to add **nutrients** to the soil. These nutrients then feed their crops. The ancient Egyptians grew all their crops on the flood plains of the River Nile. They believed that a god called Hapy controlled the Nile floods.

Flash floods

Sometimes though, floods can be very sudden and unexpected. These floods are called **flash floods**. They usually occur after very heavy rain has fallen in a very short period of time, or after dams on rivers or lakes suddenly break and release vast quantities of water very rapidly.

Sea-water floods

Sea water can be just as dangerous as heavy rain or flash floods if it pounds coasts or surges up rivers. When sea-water flooding is caused by strong winds or high tides, it can usually be predicted a few hours before it occurs. Tide levels depend on the positions of the sun, moon and earth, so they can be worked out in advance. Weather forecasting usually gives several hours warning of very strong winds. However, when

FLOOD LEGENDS

Many ancient peoples told stories about a gigantic flood that covered the whole earth. The well-known tale of Noah's Ark is based on a story that came from ancient Mesopotamia (modern Iraq) more than 3,000 years ago. Similar stories were being told in the Middle East, Greece and India 500 years later. In all these stories, one man is warned that the earth will be flooded, so he and his family build a boat and live in it until the floods subside.

earthquakes beneath the sea create enormous waves called **tsunamis**, there is often no time to warn people living along the nearest coasts.

This is the flooded town of Cockermouth, Cumbria, United Kingdom, in November 2009, after 30 centimetres of rain fell in 24 hours.

COPING WITH A FLOOD

The speed and weight of moving water makes a flood incredibly dangerous. Floods can sweep away houses, bridges, trees and cars. If people and animals cannot get out of a flood's path, they are swept away, too.

> ' I could see a huge wall advancing . . . it was a dark mass in which <u>seethed</u> houses, freight cars, trees and animals . . . my boyhood home was crushed like an eggshell before my eyes.'
>
> *Victor Heiser, flood survivor in Johnstown, Pennsylvania, 1889.*

The effects of flooding

Often serious flooding leaves people homeless, without shelter, drinking water or food. Another big problem is that flood water may become polluted with **sewage**, the dead bodies of people and animals and poisonous chemicals, all of which pose health risks.

Preparing to leave

People who live in areas at risk from flooding should have an action plan ready for when floods are predicted. They need

Flood water is very destructive, even inside houses. It can not only wreck furniture and carpets but also break windows and destroy plaster walls and ceilings.

This car has been picked up and overturned by river flood water. Large, solid objects and tree branches in fast-flowing water can hurt or even kill people swept away by a flood.

to know where they will go if they have to leave their homes and they should collect supplies of drinking water and canned food to take with them.

If a flood is predicted, it is important to bring indoors anything that might get swept away. Heavy objects carried along in fast-flowing water are extremely dangerous. Before leaving the house, gas, electricity and water should be turned off.

Many people think that they can escape in a car, but this is only a good idea if there is plenty of time to get out of the danger area or drive to higher ground. People are often trapped in cars. Just 60 centimetres of water can sweep a car away.

'I was thinking I was going to drown.'

AMAZING ESCAPE

Saved by a log

In 1990, heavy rain flooded streams near Shadyside, Ohio, in the United States. A wall of water, mud and **debris** swept through the town, killing 26 people. Nine-year-old Amber Colvin climbed into the bathtub, thinking she'd be safe. The water broke down the bathroom door and swept the tub up to the ceiling. As the ceiling gave way, she was flung into the raging waters. Amber managed to grab onto a passing log. She clung to it for seven hours as she was swept into and down the Ohio River. Amber later told reporters: 'I went under twice . . . I swallowed water and choked. I was thinking I was going to drown.' Eventually she drifted to shore, 11 kilometres down the river.

HEAVY RAIN AND RIVER FLOODS

Most floods are caused by heavy, continuous rainfall or by melting snow in spring. This water is usually absorbed by the soil, but sometimes the soil is already **saturated** by previous rainfall. In this case, the water runs straight off into rivers and streams, which fill up then overflow.

In England in July 2007 the historic centre of Tewkesbury, around its abbey, became an island in a sea of flood water.

Tewkesbury floods

The worst flooding often occurs where streams or rivers join together. This happened when floods devastated parts of the United Kingdom in 2007 after weeks of heavy rain. In Tewkesbury the River Avon meets Britain's longest river, the Severn. As the rivers overflowed, the town centre flooded and some children were trapped in their school overnight. The **waterworks** were flooded, too, leaving people without drinking water.

Floods in southern Africa

In 2000, countries in southern Africa – especially Mozambique – were hit by floods that followed the heaviest rain in the region for forty years. Rivers overflowed their banks and flooded farmland and villages. Many people survived by climbing onto the roofs of their houses or into trees. They had to wait for many days without food or drinking water before they were rescued by helicopter or boat.

'None of us could sleep in case we fell into the water.'

Cesar Messingue, who escaped the flood water by climbing into a tree, Mozambique, 2000.

HELPING HANDS

In flood disasters, aid agencies and **charities** help the people who are affected. In Mozambique, some organizations set up camps of tents to provide shelter for people who had abandoned their homes. In these camps the charity Save the Children worked non-stop to reunite lost children with their parents.

Other aid agencies fought outbreaks of diseases with **antibiotics**. Some diseases were caused by the polluted water and others by mosquito bites. Mosquitoes often gather in huge numbers at **stagnant** pools of water left behind by floods.

After the floods receded, people moved back to their villages. The Red Cross provided tents and plastic sheets for shelter, blankets for warmth and seeds to plant. Seeds were important because they would grow into crops that could be harvested later in the same year.

Women wade through the streets of Maputo in Mozambique, trying to lead a normal life. The danger is that this water is already polluted and will bring disease to the people of the city.

'It looked like a giant waterslide.'

MIDWEST, USA JUNE 2008

During June 2008, the Midwest of the United States experienced some of the worst floods ever recorded in the region. These floods followed a wet winter and spring, which left the ground saturated around the Upper Mississippi and Ohio rivers and their **tributaries**.

In Wisconsin in 2008, flood water washed away the earth barrier between Lake Delton and the Wisconsin River and destroyed five houses.

'It looked like a giant waterslide, but it was just coming so fast around that bend. It was just amazing.'
Dione Leonhardt

'Boats upside down, pontoon boats floating down the river. The next thing we saw was a house.'
Robert Dorn

'There's no way we could stop it. The volume of water was so great there wasn't anything anyone could do.'
Thomas Diehl

As the water in Lake Delton poured out, it carved a passageway to the Wisconsin River, completely washing away a section of road that was in its path.

Volunteers in Afton, Minnesota, 1997, attempt to strengthen a levee with plastic and sandbags alongside a river swollen by heavy rain.

Failing levees

In early June, more rain fell over the Midwest. It was clear that many **levees** (barriers) would break under the weight of the water. Thousands of people filled sandbags and placed them on levees and around their homes to try to halt the rushing waters. One Illinois resident told reporters: 'We heard the sirens . . . and someone said the levee just broke . . . about 20 minutes later, the whole street was just full of water.'

Flood damage

Many towns and large areas of farmland were flooded. In the city of Cedar Rapids, Iowa, the river swept away a railway bridge, along with the loaded railway carriages that had been left on the bridge in an attempt to prevent the river from carrying the bridge away.

ARE LEVEES A GOOD IDEA?

People in the Midwest live and farm on flood plains because they have built a system of levees to control river floods. Levees are artificial, sloping earth walls alongside rivers. A levee prevents a river from spilling onto the flood plain, but after heavy rainfall the water has no alternative but to rise higher and flow faster. In severe floods, the water eventually rises enough to overflow or break through levees further down the river.

After the flooding, the American Red Cross provided food and clean-up kits for thousands of people whose homes and towns had been flooded. Many people's homes and businesses were so badly affected that the US Federal Emergency Management Agency (FEMA) gave or lent large sums of money to repair the damage. Even with this help, recovery in the region took weeks and even months. Farming was hit very hard, too. The Midwest is an important corn- and soya bean-growing region, and much of the year's crop was lost in the floods.

CYCLONES AND HURRICANES

Tropical cyclones – also called hurricanes or typhoons – are rotating (circling) storm systems that begin to form over the oceans near the **equator** and then move north or south. When a cyclone reaches a coast its exceptionally strong winds cause **storm surges** that flood coastal areas. As the cyclone moves inland it produces heavy rain that can cause even more flooding.

*In August 2009, Taiwan was hit by typhoon Morakot, the deadliest in its history. More than 500 people died in the flooding and **mudslides** triggered by the heavy rain. In this photo some of the residents of Chiatung have been rescued from their homes.*

The deadliest cyclones

The deadliest cyclone ever recorded hit the Ganges River delta in India and East Pakistan (now Bangladesh) in 1970. Storm surges drowned thousands of people on low-lying coasts and islands. Five years later, Typhoon Nina swept over China, bringing torrential rain to inland regions. Many dams broke under the weight of the water, causing flash floods that killed about 100,000 people.

Hurricane Katrina

In August 2005, storm surges caused by Hurricane Katrina brought massive destruction and flooding to the Gulf Coast of the United States. The city of New Orleans, Louisiana, was in the hurricane's path. New Orleans lies on coastal swampland, mostly below sea level, so a system of levees had been built around it. The mayor of New Orleans ordered the evacuation of the city.

When the hurricane passed through the city, an 8.5-metre-high storm surge broke through 53 levees. Eighty per cent of New Orleans was flooded. Some areas were submerged under six metres of water. Over the next few days, the Coast Guard and the National Guard rescued the people left in the city.

In all, about 700 people died. Later, the disaster was analyzed to see what had gone wrong. It became clear the levees had not been effective. Now the levee system around New Orleans is being rebuilt to a much higher standard.

Vast areas of New Orleans were flooded after Hurricane Katrina. Thousands of people were trapped in their homes or on rooftops, waiting to be rescued by boat or helicopter.

'We could hear people left behind screaming for help from rooftops. We routinely heard gunshots as people trapped on rooftops tried to get the attention of helicopters criss-crossing the skies above.'

Bill Quigley, a lawyer trapped in a hospital in the New Orleans flood.

LEFT BEHIND

Despite the evacuation order, 60,000 people were left stranded in New Orleans. Public transport had been shut down, and the city government failed to provide transport for people without cars. Those left in the city included patients, their families and staff in hospitals, elderly people in nursing homes, disabled people and people in prisons.

TSUNAMIS AND HIGH TIDES

Of all sea-water floods, those caused by tsunamis are the most unexpected and destructive. Tsunamis are huge shock waves, which are usually triggered by underwater earthquakes and volcanoes. Occasionally, large **landslides** into the sea also cause tsunamis. A tsunami can travel for long distances across an ocean without losing much of its energy. As it nears a coast and the ground rises, the wave slows down and becomes higher and more deadly.

Towns on the west coast of Thailand were badly damaged by the Indian Ocean tsunami in 2004. Patong is a popular holiday area and many people died on the beaches when the tsunami swept in.

Indian Ocean catastrophe

In 2004, a massive earthquake under the Indian Ocean near Indonesia triggered a tsunami that spread across the ocean as far as Africa. At least 200,000 people died, mainly in Indonesia, Thailand, India and Sri Lanka, as waves up to 30 metres high swept through coastal communities.

'A seething mass of boiling water, crowned by a white crest came round the shore . . . it sent speedboats flying around the tops of the waves like matchsticks.'

Temmy Maclean, on holiday in Thailand.

North Sea disaster

Coastal flooding usually occurs when high tides and storm winds push sea water over the coast and up **estuaries**. In 1953, a storm surge in the North Sea caused widespread floods in coastal areas of eastern England and the Netherlands. More than 1,600 people died as the sea crashed over their houses during the night. In one of the earliest ever helicopter rescue missions, the British Navy flew helicopters to the Netherlands to drop supplies to the homeless and pick up people who had been stranded by the floods.

The historic centre of Venice is occasionally flooded by sea water. The people in Venice are used to these minor tidal floods, but occasionally the flood water can be as deep as 1.5 metres.

CITY UNDER WATER

The historic city of Venice sits on small islands in shallow water at the edge of the Adriatic Sea in north-eastern Italy. The city experiences mild floods regularly, but worse floods can occur between autumn and spring, when seasonal winds make the tides higher. In the 20th century, water was extracted from the ground around Venice for use in local industries. As a result, Venice began to sink, so high tides became even higher.

The government of Venice is now constructing inflatable gates on the seabed where the shallow water meets the deeper Adriatic Sea. These gates will be pumped full of air before very high tides. When they are fully inflated they should prevent the incoming tide from flooding Venice.

MONSOON FLOODS

Every year, from June to September, a wind called a monsoon blows over India, Pakistan, Bangladesh and Nepal. The monsoon brings heavy rain, which farmers need for their crops, but this rain also brings great misery to many regions. It floods homes and villages, drowning people and farm animals and destroying crops.

The monsoon reaches southern India and areas around the Bay of Bengal at the beginning of June. About a month later both tracks of the monsoon reach the India–Pakistan border.

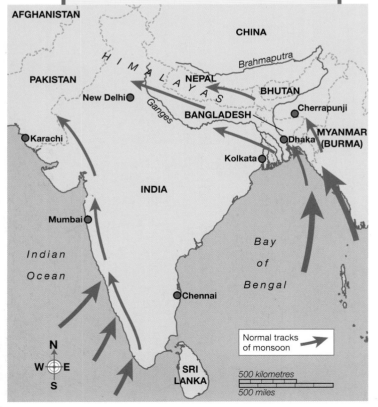

Heat and rain

Monsoon winds are triggered by the land heating up in the summer months. As the air heats up and rises, moist air is sucked in from the Indian Ocean and lifted up over the land. As the air cools it produces heavy rain.

Monsoon journey

The monsoon moves up the western coast of India, bringing rain with it. Monsoon winds also rush across the Bay of Bengal, on India's eastern side, picking up more moisture. The monsoon eventually reaches the eastern Himalayan mountains, bringing very heavy rain and flooding to north-eastern India and Bangladesh. Then it moves west over the plains of northern India.

In September, as the landmass of India begins to cool, the air changes and a cold wind sweeps south from the Himalayas, bringing with it heavy rain to much of southern India.

'It was as if the bottom had fallen out of an ocean in the sky.'

Nick Middleton describes monsoon rain in his book Going to Extremes.

THE WETTEST PLACE ON EARTH?

The hill town of Cherrapunji in north-eastern India used to be the wettest place on earth. As the monsoon sweeps in from the Bay of Bengal, the local hills are the first place to experience monsoon rains.

Today, because of **global warming**, this region of India is getting hotter and the monsoon is arriving later. In addition, the forests have been cut down, and much of the soil has been washed away. All the water that was stored in the ground now runs away downhill. Sometimes the people in one of the wettest places on earth have to travel out of their town to find drinking water.

Monsoon flooding hit Dhaka, Bangladesh, in July 2009. People who were not trapped in their flooded homes struggled to get to work in a variety of ways. Here rickshaw pullers and cyclists fight their way through the water.

'There were many poisonous snakes in the water.'

BANGLADESH AND INDIA 2007

People in India and Bangladesh tell their stories after the 2007 monsoon.

'Everything is underwater. We've lost our crops, there's nowhere to put the children down, not even a place to cook.'
Musamat Manwara Khatoum, villager in Bangladesh

'Our family survived for a week on buffalo milk, but now the animal has stopped producing milk as it has gone without food for days.'
Meghu Yadav, villager in India

'When we were going by boat to remote villages at night there were many poisonous snakes in the water. From villages surrounded by water we heard the pathetic cries of women and children.'
Hamid Raza, aid worker in India

In 2007 the worst monsoon anyone had experienced for many years caused widespread devastation and suffering across southern Asia. In India alone, 3,500 people died and two million homes were destroyed.

Mud and water

In the port city of Chittagong in Bangladesh, the rains caused mudslides as well as floods. Across Bangladesh and northern India, rivers overflowed their banks, leaving people stranded on islands and higher ground. Many people had to climb onto the roofs of their houses or into trees to escape the waters.

These two Bangladeshi village women are forced to walk through the flood waters to shop for food and essential items.

THE PLIGHT OF BANGLADESH

Most of Bangladesh lies on the flood plains of rivers which begin their journey high up in the Himalayas. In Bangladesh, these rivers form the Ganges **delta**. In late spring and summer, the snow melts in the Himalayas. All this water fills the rivers, which flood over the flat, low-lying areas of Bangladesh. Bursting rivers are not the only flooding problem the country faces. Much of Bangladesh is less than one metre above sea level. This leaves it exposed to cyclones, which cause coastal flooding.

Stranded in the floods

Aid agencies tried desperately to get food, drinking water, materials for shelters and medicine to the millions of people stranded in the southern Asian floods. Helicopters rescued people and dropped food supplies for isolated communities. Many people had only polluted flood water to drink or cook with, so they were suffering from diseases such as **cholera** and **dysentery**.

*Indian villagers on an **embankment** above the flood water collect supplies that have been dropped by helicopter.*

FLASH FLOODS

Flash floods strike very quickly. Usually a thunderstorm stays over a small area of high ground and produces massive amounts of rain for just a few hours. So much rain falls in such a short period of time that the ground cannot absorb it all. The water runs off and collects in low-lying areas. Flash floods are very dangerous for people living at the bottom of valleys. The narrower the channel the water flows through, the faster it flows and the more damage it does.

In August 1997 rain storms in the United States caused a flash flood through the narrow Antelope Gorge in Colorado. Brown, foaming water full of trees and boulders raced down the canyon and killed 12 tourists. They were only metres away from ladders that could have taken them out of the canyon.

In September 2009 a flash flood swept through the city of Istanbul, Turkey, killing more than 20 people. This local flood was so severe that it overturned and destroyed parked lorries.

'Every time I close my eyes I see that water.'

This home in Minnesota in the United States was swept onto railway tracks by the force of a flash flood in 2007.

AMAZING ESCAPE

Up the canyon wall

On the evening of 31 July 1976, emergency medics John McMaster and George Woodson were driving their ambulance up Big Thompson Canyon, Colorado, to answer an emergency call. Suddenly an enormous wave covered the road and lifted their vehicle four metres above the ground. Both men somehow climbed out of the ambulance window, then grabbed the canyon wall and scrambled up it. When a rock came loose, McMaster fell nine metres. He just managed to cling on to the canyon wall with his body in the water. When dawn came and the water level fell, the two men climbed down to the canyon floor and were rescued by a helicopter. 'I just can't figure how we climbed out of those windows,' McMaster said. 'Every time I close my eyes I see that water.'

A flash flood can also devastate a much wider area. In August 2007 cold air from Canada and warm, wet air from the Gulf of Mexico collided over the Midwestern United States, producing record amounts of rain. For example, in some areas of Minnesota 40 centimetres of rain fell in 24 hours. In the flash floods that followed, 18 people died. One official reported that 'Some people had to cut holes in their roofs to get out.'

'There were cars all around us at sea.'

BOSCASTLE, CORNWALL, UNITED KINGDOM 16 AUGUST 2004

Andrew Cameron, crew member of the Port Isaac lifeboat.

'We were the first lifeboat on the scene and were greeted by a 10–15 foot [3–4.5 metre] wall of water coming down the town, out of the harbour and pushing 30, maybe 50 cars in front of it. There were cars all around us at sea, there was debris everywhere, the air was thick with the stench of fuel. Then another storm came in as we arrived, so lightning was hitting all around us. There were about seven helicopters in the air. The rain was so heavy you couldn't see right in front of you.'

Boscastle is an ancient coastal village on the north coast of Cornwall in south-western England. It sits at the bottom of a steep, narrow river valley. On the afternoon of 16 August 2004, 18.5 centimetres of rain fell on the hills inland from the village. In Boscastle itself, almost nine centimetres were recorded in one hour. All this rain fell on a very small area. A few kilometres away, there was very little rain at all.

A rescue helicopter flies over Boscastle as water rages through the village down to the sea.

'There were 60-foot [18-metre] trees just going down the river like matchsticks.'

Alan Graham, trapped on the roof of the visitor centre in Boscastle.

Swept into the sea

River levels rose two metres in just one hour, and the steep-sided valley acted like a giant funnel. A three-metre-high wave swept down the road, carrying trees and debris with it and causing massive damage. Six buildings collapsed, and about 50 cars were washed into the harbour. Many people were stranded in cars, trees, or on rooftops and had to be rescued by helicopter. Amazingly, no-one died in the flood.

One tourist said: 'I watched cars being picked up like toys. Roads were lifted up and crashed down onto cars like the jaws of a monster.'

BOSCASTLE AND LYNMOUTH

Fifty-two years to the day before the Boscastle flood, another flood devastated the coastal village of Lynmouth, in Devon, about 100 kilometres to the east. The two floods were very similar. Lynmouth is also at the bottom of a steep, narrow valley where two rivers meet, and 23 centimetres of rain had fallen on high ground above the village in less than a day. Unfortunately, the people in Lynmouth were not as lucky as those in Boscastle: 34 people died.

This 1952 postcard shows the damage caused by the swollen River Lyn as it raced through the seaside town of Lynmouth.

MANMADE FLOODS

In the last hundred years, human activities have made many floods worse. In some cases they have actually caused flooding. Attempts to tame rivers have also often had the opposite effect. As river ecologist David Galat points out, humans are interfering with natural events: 'A flood is not a disturbance of a river. The absence of a flood is a disturbance of a river.'

Protecting flood plains

Flood plains are flat areas, which makes them good places to build houses and other buildings. In order to build on a flood plain, people first have to restrict the river's flow. This can be done safely if the dams and levees they build do not give way under the weight of the water. If they do break, towns are suddenly flooded.

Problems in towns

The materials used to build towns often make flooding worse. Soil is replaced by concrete and tarmac, which do not soak up water. When a town is flooded, the water remains on the surface. Rain runs off the roofs of houses, the roads become rivers, and lakes form in the lowest-lying areas. Drains cannot cope with these amounts of water. It spills into sewage systems, washing the sewage out to pollute the flood water, which often lies around for several days.

Cologne, one of the largest cities built along the Rhine, was one of many places badly flooded in 1995.

PROBLEMS ALONG THE RHINE

The River Rhine is one of Europe's longest rivers. In 1995, the Rhine and its tributaries flooded areas of France, Belgium, the Netherlands and Germany. The floods were made worse by the following human activities.

- Forests in the Alps – where the Rhine begins its journey – have been cut down. The rainwater that used to be taken up by the trees now runs off the surface into the rivers. In addition, soil is washed into the river, reducing its depth.

- Towns have been built on 60 per cent of the flood plain, which once absorbed rainwater. Now rainwater flows off roofs and roads into drains that lead directly to the river.

- Embankments have been raised to protect towns and industrial areas. These keep flood water in the river, causing worse floods further downstream.

- Parts of the Rhine have been straightened so that large barges can use it. This has shortened the river, so the same amount of water flows much faster. Fast-flowing rivers are more likely to flood.

After the River Rhine leaves the Swiss Alps it flows past several large cities – and many smaller ones – before forming a delta in the Netherlands.

FLOODS AND GLOBAL WARMING

The temperature of the earth has been rising rapidly for around fifty years. Most scientists now think that this global warming is the result of burning **fossil fuels** such as oil and coal. As they burn, fossil fuels give off gases which remain in the atmosphere and stop heat escaping from the planet.

Ice turns to water

Global warming is already melting polar ice caps and mountain **glaciers**. The ice turns to water that ends up in the oceans. As a result, sea levels rise. Some scientists predict that sea levels will rise between 60 and 100 centimetres by the year 2100. If this happens, many areas that are now near sea level will be permanently flooded.

Areas at risk

Many low-lying islands are at risk. In Asia, coasts where millions of people live will also flood more frequently. In the United States, parts of southern Florida, the Mississippi Delta in Louisiana and the North Carolina coast may vanish under the Atlantic Ocean. In Britain, eastern England around The Wash is already only just above sea level.

Penguins gather on a chunk of ice which has just broken away from a melting glacier in the Southern Ocean – a sign that global warming is taking place.

The tiny island of Guraidhoo in the Maldives was swamped by the Indian Ocean tsunami in 2004 and many of its houses were flattened.

Warmer air, more rain

As the sea level rises, the sea water will enter river estuaries. This will make it harder for river water to enter the sea, so people living on estuaries will face more flooding. Global warming will also change air patterns, perhaps leading to more extreme weather events such as storms and hurricanes, so severe flooding further inland is also likely to become more common.

> ' Warmer air can hold more moisture, so heavier precipitation [rainfall] is expected in the years to come.'
>
> Amanda Staudt, climate scientist.

A SPECK IN THE OCEAN

The Maldives is a group of hundreds of islands in the middle of the Indian Ocean. Its highest point is only 2.3 metres above sea level. By the year 2100, there will be very little of the Maldives left, and its 360,000 people will be forced to leave. Already some people want to move elsewhere because high tides flood their homes every two weeks. The president of the Maldives, Mohammed Nasheed has said: 'We have to buy land elsewhere . . . we do not want to be climate refugees living in tents for decades.'

FLOOD PREVENTION

People try to prevent or control floods in a number of ways. Dams hold water behind a barrier and release it slowly. Dikes, levees and embankments are all walls that prevent water from escaping. Drainage channels leading away from rivers are dug to divert excess water to places where it will cause no damage. Along coasts, walls and artificial islands act as barriers to keep sea damage to a minimum.

Protecting the Netherlands

The Netherlands takes flood defences very seriously because much of the country lies below sea level. In 1932 a 32-kilometre-long, 7.2-metre-high dam was built between the provinces of North Holland and Friesland. Parts of the North Sea trapped behind it were then drained and turned into farmland, forests and towns. Later in the 20th century, the Dutch constructed dams and storm surge barriers on estuaries of the Rhine delta to block or restrict tidal flows.

' [Flood defences are] not cheap . . . [but they are] a kind of insurance.'

' [In the Netherlands] if something goes wrong, ten million people can be threatened.'

Tjalle de Haan, Dutch government engineer.

A traditional dike in the Netherlands protects this house against flooding from the sea. As well as these old-style dikes, the Netherlands has a hi-tech system of flood defences.

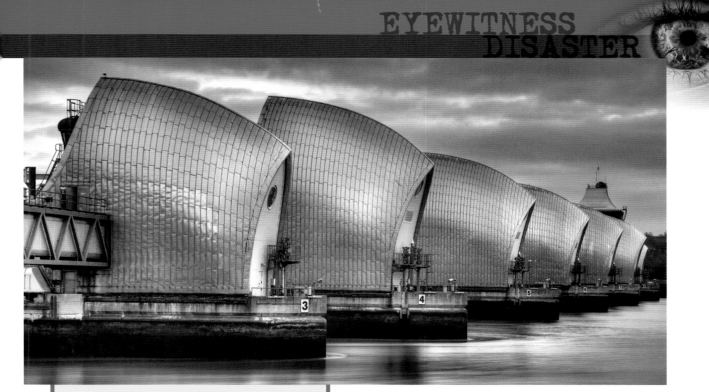

The concrete piers of the Thames Barrier in London support the underwater barriers which are only raised when flooding is threatened.

Nature and floods

Today scientists realize that nature can play a part in the fight against floods. In China, forests are being planted to keep the soil in place and soak up water. After disastrous flooding in the Midwest in 1993, the United States government decided to move thousands of people away from flood plains and recreate **wetlands** along the rivers. The vegetation that grows in the wetlands soaks up water like a sponge, reducing the flooding in the area around it.

As the 21st century progresses – and sea levels rise and severe storms become more common – many more artificial and natural flood defences will be needed to prevent disastrous floods.

THAMES BARRIER

Between 1974 and 1982 the Thames Barrier was built across the River Thames to protect the city of London, England, from very high tides and sea surges. Hollow, curved, steel barriers lie between concrete **piers** which contain the mechanism that works the barriers. Most of the time the barriers are totally submerged in a concrete cradle on the river bed. They can be rotated 90 degrees before high tides to form a shield against the incoming sea.

GLOSSARY

antibiotics drugs that kill bacteria

charity an organization that helps people in need

cholera an infection that causes diarrhoea

debris the remains of broken or destroyed objects

delta the wide area of land and waterways at the mouth of a river where it meets the sea

dysentery an infection that causes diarrhoea

embankment an artificial earth wall built to provide a route across a wet area or to stop flooding

equator the imaginary circle around the earth which is halfway between both poles and which is the boundary between the northern and southern hemispheres

estuary the lowest part of a river where it meets tidal water from the sea

flash flood a sudden flood usually caused by heavy rainfall that lasts for only a few hours

flood plain flat land next to a river

fossil fuels fuels, such as oil, coal and gas, which are created when organisms die and break down (decompose) in an oxygen-free environment

glacier a slow-moving mass of ice which is formed from layers of crushed snow

global warming the increase in the temperature of the air and oceans that has been happening since at least the mid 20th century

landslide a fast-moving mass of rock or debris down a slope

levee a slope or wall parallel to a river, built to prevent flooding

mudslide a movement downhill of mud formed from loose soil and water

nutrient a substance that living organisms need to live and grow

pier a structure built in water but rising above the surface

saturated unable to absorb any more moisture

seethe move in a violent, agitated way

sewage human waste carried away in water

stagnant describes water that is not flowing and may be full of bacteria

storm surge a sea-water rise caused by high winds pressing on the ocean surface

tributary a stream or river that flows into a larger stream or river

tsunami a series of sea waves caused by an undersea earthquake, volcano or landslide

waterworks a place where water is stored, purified and pumped to where it is needed

wetland an area of land either covered by water or with very wet soil

FURTHER INFORMATION

Books

Chambers, Catherine, *Flood (Wild Weather)*, Heinemann Library, 2007

Connolly, Sean, *Flood (In Time of Need)*, Franklin Watts, 2004

Ganeri, Anita, *Flood (Nature's Fury)*, Franklin Watts, 2006

Guillain, Charlotte, *Protect our Planet – Global Warming (Polluted Planet)*, Heinemann Library, 2008

Harman, Rebecca, *The Earth's Weather (Heinemann Infosearch: Earth's Processes)*, Heinemann Library, 2005

McCarthy, Shaun, *Raging Floods (Heinemann Infosearch)*, Heinemann Library, 2004

Pipe, Jim, *Weather and Climate (Planet Earth)*, ticktock Media Ltd., 2008

DVD

Natural Disasters, DK Eyewitness Books, 2009

Websites

There are many websites that tell you about floods. These are just some:

http://apps.sepa.org.uk/floodlinekids/index.html
The Scottish Environment Protection Agency This site includes the causes of flooding and preparing for floods.

http://earthobservatory.nasa.gov/NaturalHazards/
NASA's web site provides satellite images of floods.

http://search.bbc.co.uk/search?order=sortboth&q=floods&x=19&y=9&scope=cnews&tab=cnews
CBBC newsround articles about flooding around the world include children's experiences.

http://science.howstuffworks.com/flood.htm
The Earth Science pages include 'How Floods work' and 'Was There Really a Great Flood?'

www.bbc.co.uk/devon/content/articles/2007/07/03/lynmouth_floods_archive_video_feature.shtml
The black and white news film of the 1952 Lynmouth flood disaster contains interviews.

http://www.bbc.co.uk/weather/features/understanding/1953_flood.shtml
The 1953 East Coast Floods. What caused them and what happened afterwards.

http://www.fema.gov/kids/floods/floods.htm
The US Federal Emergency Management Agency explains how to prepare for flooding and what to do in an evacuation.

http://www.jaha.org/FloodMuseum/history.html
The story of the Johnstown, Pennsylvania, flood of 1889 in detail, plus many stories from survivors.

http://www.metoffice.gov.uk/education/teens/casestudy_floods.html
The story of the 1953 East Coast floods from Met Office Education.

http://www.metoffice.gov.uk/education/teens/casestudy_boscastle.html
This Met office site looks in detail at what happened in Boscastle.

http://www.pbs.org/newshour/infocus/floods.html
This site includes 'Real Life Accounts', 'Flood Fighters', 'Pet Rescues' , 'Grand Forks Recovers', plus the science of floods and audio stories.

http://www.rapidcitylibrary.org/lib_info/1972Flood/index.asp
Photos, facts, interviews and memories from the Rapid City flood of 1972.

INDEX

aid agencies 9, 11, 19
Afton, Minnesota 11
Antelope Gorge, Colorado 20
Avon, River 8

Bangladesh 12, 16, 17, 18–19
Big Thompson Canyon, Colorado 21
Boscastle, Cornwall 22–23

Cedar Rapids, Iowa 11
Cherrapunji, India 17
Chiatung, Taiwan 12
China 12, 29
Chittagong, Bangladesh 18
coastal flooding 4–5, 12, 14, 15, 19, 26, 27
Cockermouth, Cumbria 5
Cologne, Germany 24
cyclones 12–13, 19

dams 4, 12, 24, 28
Delton, Lake 10
Dhaka, Bangladesh 17
dikes 28
diseases 9, 19
drinking water 6, 7, 8, 17, 19

earthquakes, underwater 5, 14
embankments 25, 28

flash floods 4, 12, 20–21, 22–23
flood plains 4, 11, 19, 24, 25, 29
flood prevention 15, 28–29

Ganges, River 12, 19
global warming 17, 26–27

Himalayas 16, 19
Hurricane Katrina 12–13
hurricanes 12–13, 27

India 5, 12, 14, 16, 17, 18, 19
Indian Ocean 14, 16, 27
Istanbul, Turkey 20

Johnstown, Pennsylvania 6

levees 12–13, 24, 28
Lynmouth, Devon 23

Maldives 27
Maputo, Mozambique 9
Midwest, USA 10–11, 21, 29
Minnesota 11, 21
Mississippi River 10, 26
monsoon 16–17, 18–19
Mozambique 8, 9

Netherlands 14, 25, 28
New Orleans, Louisiana 12–13
Nile, River 4
Noah's Ark 5
North Sea 14, 28

Ohio River 7, 10
Ouagadougou, Burkina Faso 4

polluted water 6, 9, 19, 24

Rhine, River 24, 25, 28

saturated soil 8, 10, 20
sea levels, rising 26–27, 29
Severn, River 8
Shadyside, Ohio 7
storm surges 12, 14

Taiwan 12
Tewkesbury 8
Thailand 14
Thames Barrier 29
tides 4, 5 14–15, 27, 29
tsunamis 5, 14, 27
typhoons 12–13

Venice, Italy 15
volcanoes, underwater 14

Wash, The 26
Wisconsin River 10